DAILY EXPRESS and SUNDAY EXPRESS Cartoons

Fifty Ninth Series

Giles characters™ and © 2005 Express Newspapers

Published By Express Newspapers, Number 10 Lower Thames Street, London EC3R 6EN

ISBN 0-850793-07-6

An Introduction by

Jim Bowen

I happen to be one of the huge silent majority in the UK who internally rages at the stupid inequalities that this great democracy of ours portends to protect. We, none of us dare speak out because we take the easy option.

Herein lies the enormous value of 'Giles'. He shamelessly ridicules the do-gooder, the interfering politically correct imbecile who irritates us beyond belief, and then uses his artistic, observant humorous talents to present his case visually to a massive readership that enjoys the Daily Express.

There are not many cartoonists who can actually raise a guffaw of delight from yours truly, so I write this foreword with great pleasure as it gives me a tangible opportunity to say :- "Thanks Giles, for putting into glorious pictures the many frustrating thoughts this society of ours initiates, but dare not talk about with too much enthusiasm".

Trust me dear reader, as a broadcaster for the BBC for some years I do have the T-shirt to comment with authority!

You will enjoy this publication.

JIM BOWEN

The Long Arm of the Law

"Just what I expected. Do as Gaitskell says and give 'em lifts and get yourself pulled for joy riding."

Sunday Express, January 18, 1948

"It's all right, officer – merely putting a Christmas present from an aunt where I know where it is."

Sunday Express, December 26, 1948

"Now if you send that slogan in to the Express and win ten guineas, it'll just about pay your fine."

Daily Express, January 14, 1950

"Break it up, girls – the cops!"

Daily Express, June 22, 1950

"Private Hoggswhistle, sir. Wishes to know whether his strong Left-wing tendencies will cause him to be banned from leaving the country with the battalion next week."

Daily Express, July 24, 1951

"But I read in the papers yesterday that they let a man off for playing a mouth organ while he was driving."

Daily Express, August 14, 1952

"If we had a State Opening of Parliament back home, at least our cops'd let us throw tickertape."

Daily Express, November 3, 1953

"Dad! You know Grandma said she'd like to tell one of these cops what she thinks of them before we went home?"

Daily Express, October 5, 1962

"Bunch of 'em for the Smithfield – been in there all the afternoon."

Daily Express, December 4, 1962

"Nice work, lads – ninety-four demonstrators, one King, H.R.H., three bus conductors ..."

Daily Express, July 11, 1963

"I'm not dead – but I've got a ticket and I'll be killed in the rush if the others find out."

Daily Express, October 29, 1963

"Madam, we could accept your story that your boy painted them but for the coincidence that he has painted exactly one hundred and nineteen."

Daily Express, February 3, 1976

"You've read the notice, Madam – do you still claim that P. C. Boggis deliberately kicked your little Pamela?"

Daily Express, October 14, 1976

"If they can lose something the size of Idi Amin, you're making a lot of fuss about losing two small tickets."

Daily Express, June 22, 1977

"No doubt Her Majesty will be most touched tomorrow by your patriotic devotion. Now get the bloody thing off!"

Daily Express, June 27, 1977

"Why don't you escape, kill a railway guard, make a record, and be a punk hero overnight?"

Daily Express, August 8, 1978

"The Prosecution claims this lady did throw a cabbage at her neighbour's poodle who was trespassing upon her lawn. How the devil did this get to the High Court?"

Daily Express, December 7, 1978

"You saw her unprovoked attack and you didn't raise a bloody finger in our defence!"

Daily Express, January 11, 1979

"Tell that woman the court is only concerned where the defendant was on the night of the crime, not what he thinks of Fergie's latest hat."

Daily Express, April 7, 1988

"The judge didn't let me off because I've got a baby – but I get time off for his good behaviour."

Daily Express, January 7, 1990

Sporting Pursuits

"After all, Uncle – it's only a game of bat and ball."

Daily Express, January 11, 1951

"I ain't loitering – I've fallen head over tip."

Daily Express, April 18, 1951

"We could tell the young gentleman the winner for Saturday if we wasn't so dry, couldn't we, Sidney?"

Daily Express, April 3, 1952

"They're bound to effect our gate a little bit, Cyril."

Daily Express, April 27, 1954

"We'll have to lower their entrance price out of our tax relief – we're getting more 'boos' than the ref ..."

Daily Express, April 11, 1957

"Can't you keep your confounded women out of sight?"

Daily Express, March 25, 1958

"At least it's put some life in the blessed game."

Sunday Express, April 10, 1960

"Please can we have our ball?"

Daily Express, May 10, 1963

"What's the score?"

Daily Express, July 28, 1964

"Ladies, PLEASE! Come, let us have no World Cup tactics – it is the glory of the game that counts."

Sunday Express, July 24, 1966

"OK Lou – if you don't want a repeat of this get in there, mingle unobtrusively and pick up the player's form."

Daily Express, June 20, 1975

"I wish you hadn't won two tickets for the Muhammad Ali fight in Kuala Lumpur – we can hear him from back home, anyway."

Daily Express, July 1, 1975

"We love ya, baby. You've just saved racing and the Jockey Club – your 'orse lost."

Daily Express, June 1, 1977

"Unlike other judges in the news, young lady, I am not prepared to overlook your misdemeanours to benefit your promising career."

Daily Express, June 21, 1977

"Never mind whether I'm a Bjorn Borg or a Legs Lloyd fan – get out of my seat!"

Daily Express, June 26, 1978

"Robert is so against sending athletes to Moscow on principle, I wish he would apply his principles to St. Botolph's Fete."

Sunday Express, May 25, 1980

"Tell Captain Hornblower if he buys one, he'll be doing the washing up."

Daily Express, January 10, 1984

"We certainly will not call in Bob Geldof for advice on how to feed him."

Daily Express, July 31, 1986

Spot the Difference

Find 10 differences between this picture and the one on the page opposite.

Answers can be found on the final page of this book

Daily Express, October 3rd, 1962

Women and Children

"So – I bring him to see the sea for the first time and he says he'd sooner see
a good air raid any day."

Sunday Express, April 4, 1946

"What's it worth to you if we don't report you for wasting bread?"

Sunday Express, July 7, 1946

"Georgina, one of these foreigners has written to the Express objecting to dogs in our cafes!"

Daily Express, August 31, 1948

"You had no right to let Grandma make you volunteer for ambulance work, Vera."

Daily Express, January 16, 1951

"Dad, Georgie bought Lauren Bacall an Easter hat, but she didn't even get off the boat."

Daily Express, March 22, 1951

"I do hope that strike hasn't involved the crew, Emily."

Daily Express, July 26, 1951

"Sir! Smith says he LIKES the bad old mixed-age schools."

Daily Express, December 2, 1954

"Fellows, I have information for thee – Chalky is going to collect your National Savings after all."

Daily Express, January 10, 1956

"Oh dear! I've left my reading glasses at home."

Daily Express, April 16, 1957

"Your contribution to earning this shilling will be to
contact the outside world and tell our scoutmaster we
shall be here till the end of August."

Daily Express, April 26, 1957

"Well I don't think a nice Sunday walk around the New York Zoo is doing me more good than snoring my head off in an armchair at home."

Sunday Express, September 30, 1962

"Don't forget the fruit gums, Mum!"

Daily Express, May 9, 1963

"Blowing Bertie to smithereens isn't going to help the Socialist Party's call for more scientists, is it?"

Daily Express, October 3, 1963

"Our Vera thought she heard a baby seal calling for help."

Daily Express, December 7, 1963

"I distinctly told my husband to stand here and not move till I came back."

Sunday Express, December 15, 1963

"Trust you, Vera, to hop on the first bus that comes without checking the number."

Sunday Express, January 12, 1964

"Come in, Fred – the wife's entertaining a few Miss World candidates for tea."

Sunday Express, November 13, 1966

"I don't care is Prince Charming does strangle Cinderella on TV – nobody's going to hang the
Three Wise Men and split the loot in our school play."

Daily Express, December 8, 1966

"It's still a damn sight better looking than the one we've got next door."

Daily Express, September 7, 1976

"Sorry skipper – this able-seaman's strike is still on."

Sunday Express, September 12, 1976

"Your Bobbie's in the nick and can you lend him two hundred pounds until Thursday?"

Sunday Express, November 28, 1976

"Deep depression at top level. The greedy customers have bought up everything and haven't left anything for the January sales."

Daily Express, December 16, 1976

"You've been at the puff pastry again, Mrs Carbhoe. Guards!"

Daily Express, September 7, 1977

"I'd like to see mine come home saying he'd blown our life savings on an old cannon!"

Daily Express, December 2, 1977

"Ladies! As your MP surely we could discuss our grievances sitting round a table."

Sunday Express, February 19, 1978

"Never mind about doing it like with Travolta in 'Grease', Angela, we're doing it like with Fonteyn in 'Swan Lake'."

Sunday Express, September 17, 1978

"Just one snag – I have to ask him if I can have the car for the evening."

Daily Express, July 31, 1979

"He says if cigarettes go up today, he'll have to cut down on my video allowance."

Daily Express, March 13, 1984

"Thank the schools' new Lessons in Love – he wants to know who's been using his aftershave."

Daily Express, June 5, 1986

"You always said he'd got a good voice ... could turn out to be another Sinatra."

Daily Express, September 11, 1986

"It's my fault – I got him up early and said 'Get down the bank and get our cheque back before they cash it and don't come back without it'."

Daily Express, October 27, 1987

"I've seen it all – howling her eyes out because she's got to go off on holiday without her robot!"

Daily Express, March 31, 1988

"Enjoy yourself, Mr Chalk! Their parents have got 'em for two whole weeks!"

Daily Express, April 5, 1988

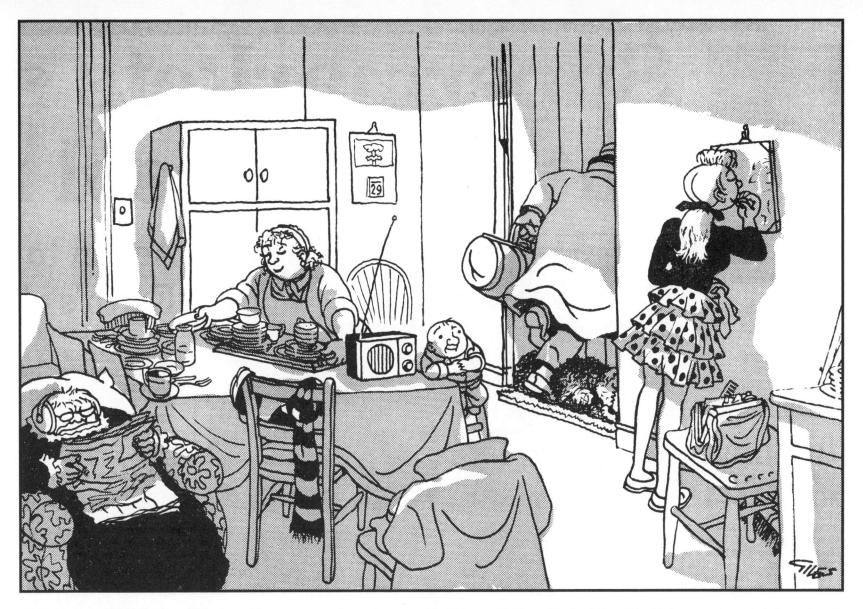

"Mixing the BBC's Royal Variety Show canned applause with Prince Philip's End of the World forecast certainly helps."

Daily Express, November 29, 1988

Society

"Perhaps this'll teach you to stay at 'ome next 'oliday."

Sunday Express, April 9, 1944

"Bah! The world's going soft sir. We managed our wars without atom bombs in my young days."

Sunday Express, February 24, 1946

"Abolishing capital punishment is simply asking for this sort of thing."

Sunday Express, April 18, 1948

"Let's have a change this Whitsun," says Father. "Let's go horse riding."

Daily Express, May 13, 1948

"Oh we've nothing to worry about – I'll steer – I know the Brighton coast like the back of my hand."

Daily Express, May 17, 1948

"I suppose if the master tailor's strike had affected Savile Row we should automatically have become a race of intellectuals."

Sunday Express, September 4, 1949

"Rather than hurt somebody's feelings, I should have been inclined to make your John Bull a bit slimmer."

Daily Express, November 21, 1951

"Decent of Ramsbotham to accept our suggestion that in an emergency he'd be the engine."

Daily Express, February 20, 1951

"Lot of wasted talent here that could be doing us a bit of good in Cortina."

Daily Express, February 2, 1956

"Lend us a couple of those balaclavas you're knitting for the troops, Vera."

Daily Express, August 8, 1956

THE FOLLOWING ENTRY HAS BEEN RECEIVED FROM GILES: BUT ALL COMPETITORS PLEASE NOTE–GILES CAN BE ABSOLUTELY GUARANTEED NOT TO BE THE WINNER

THE PERFECT NURSE
1.—Sense of humour

2.—Dependable in emergency

3.—Sense of vocation

4.—Tact

Daily Express, December 21, 1956

5.—Patience

6.—Sympathy
(see No. 2)

7.—Reassuring manner

8.—Cheerfulness
(see No. 1)

9.—Courage

10.—Gentleness

Daily Express, August 24, 1957

FAREWELL GOLDEN MILE by GILES

Concluding this pictorial record of Grandma Giles's holiday does not mean that she's had enough of Blackpool but that I've had enough of Grandma and her sister Millie for one week.
And what better place to wind up a holiday than one of those quiet, restful hostels so popular in the North. The index might help.

1. Grandma's sister explaining that if it wasn't for the bad weather and shortage of money these days the place would be packed.
2. Visitor telling Native that Blackpool's a fine place and he's coming again next year.
3. His wife thinking not if she knows it.
4. Visitor saying this Blackpool air suits him.
5. Native saying, aye, he can see that.
6. Visitor singing "Rock me baby".
7. Native from Burtonwood explaining about the American who went up 19 miles in a balloon this week.
8. Lady friend asking why Native from Burtonwood can't take her up in a balloon.
9. Another Native from Burtonwood can't take her up in a balloon.
10. Gentleman escort of No. 11 wishing everyone from Burtonwood was 19 miles up in a balloon.
11. See 10.
12. Someone singing "Galway Bay".
13. Someone singing "Will Ye No Come Back Again?".
14. Native asking piano man: "Do you know your —— row is breaking my —— eardrums?"
15. Piano man replying: "No – but if you've got the music, I'll play it." (Old joke, new version).
16. Someone singing he's a lassie from Lancashire.
17. Visitor telling barman he gave him a quid and only got change for ten bob.
18. Barman saying ——
19. Someone singing he does like to be beside the seaside.

The rest is fairly straightforward.

"Which of you lovelorn letter bashers put an ad in the local paper: 'Wanted. Eleven pretty secretaries good at answering letters'?"

Daily Express, February 7, 1963

"Careful what you spend, dear – third vase back row on your left."

Daily Express, February 25, 1975

"A very remarkable impersonation of Sir Charles Chaplin at the Palace, Guardsman Davies. After his dubbing you will receive my standing ovation in the Guardhouse."

Daily Express, March 4, 1975

"Finishing off Viscount Linley's bottle was not what headmaster meant by 'Normal way' Cholmondeley."

Daily Express, October 12, 1978

"He made their glowing colours ... He made their tiny wings ..."

Daily Express, August 9, 1979

"Never mind about the wicked British Imperialists in 1840, that egg you threw at the Queen was your Grandad's breakfast."

Daily Express, February 25, 1986

Spot the Difference

Find 10 differences between this picture and the one on the page opposite.

Answers can be found on the final page of this book

Daily Express, August 29th, 1951

A View on Politics

"If the union gets us this six bob rise, I suppose we can expect caviar and pheasant."

Sunday Express, January 20, 1946

"I suppose some top-hatted official will get the credit for this extra half pint of milk today."

Sunday Express, February 17, 1946

"What's all the fuss about? I'm democratic, aren't I? I do what I please. I say what I like.
That's democratic isn't it?"

Sunday Express, March 3, 1946

"Boy! Has that extra meat ration brought in the recruits!"

Sunday Express, September 29, 1946

"My missus took one look at these 'ere peace plans, then started cleaning me old Home Guard uniform."

Sunday Express, January 25, 1948

"Nip on and tell the Demon King he's had the smoke – we've finished our coal ration."

Sunday Express, January 9, 1949

"The lady says can we find her paper, as she thinks she voted for the wrong man."

Sunday Express, February 23, 1950

"If you won't let us use the Suez Canal, we won't let you use Battersea Park lake."

Daily Express, July 17, 1951

"If you 'ear one word out of any of 'em about nationalising all transport, 'ave 'em 'orf."

Daily Express, September 6, 1952

"The next course will be two of those UNESCO bods they sent her to find out what witch doctors' patients die of."

Daily Express, March 1, 1955

"I don't say Siberia, but they could send us to Manchester, or Birmingham or South Uist."

Daily Express, May 9, 1957

"I'm afraid we must face it, m'lady – having asked him to open our Fete as a Cabinet Minister, we're stuck with him as a back-bencher."

Daily Express, July 17, 1962

""Since they've cut his subsides, economy's gone to his head."

Sunday Express, March 17, 1963

"On my reckoning, in about a year we'll all have twenty houses each."

Daily Express, May 30, 1963

"I hope ye're no' offended, Sir Alec – my wee bairns are a wee bit radically minded."

Daily Express, November 5, 1963

"Well, apart from a few items like Rhodesia, a gas crisis, a by-election, and a rail strike threat, I don't think he's doing much this morning."

Daily Express, January 25, 1966

"There'll be a grave security risk if your name appears in the
Denning Report – yours!"

Daily Express, September 17, 1965

"I told you that bounder who asked if we'd like a ride and left us stuck up here looked a bit like Jim Callaghan."

Daily Express, October 13, 1966

"What he's really saying is 'Maggie, I know a little shop that will let you have as many crates of tinned food as you can store at 10 per cent off'."

Daily Express, February 11, 1975

"She's gone too far! Non-stop recording of 'Jerusalem' sung by the W.I. Choir!"

Daily Express, February 14, 1975

Budget Day

Daily Express, April 15, 1975

"Your demand may well be justified. However, in the meantime, we in the Diplomatic Service ..."

Daily Express, May 20, 1975

"He only promised he wouldn't speak while Margaret Thatcher was speaking."

Daily Express, October 7, 1975

"There will be a slight delay, gentlemen – she hasn't finished
wallpapering the House."

Daily Express, October 14, 1975

"I assure you there is no question of victimisation because you are Leyland workers – it's simply that we have sold out of raffle tickets."

Sunday Express, July 4, 1976

"Move along there – we've got a customer."

Daily Express, July 27, 1976

"When you've finished, I am NOT a Labour M.P. living in the lap of luxury at the expense of the unemployed – I am a redundant local government official enjoying a rather splendid roast beef and two veg. On Social Security."

Daily Express, September 28, 1976

"He's never bitten anybody before – it's just that he don't like jubilant Tories."

Sunday Express, November 7, 1976

"Anything we can do she can do better – it had to come."

Daily Express, September 7, 1978

"It's Maggie and the Cabinet. Not much else to do this year
as the Socialists did it all for them at Brighton last week."

Daily Express, October 11, 1979

"M'Lady wishes to know if you will be attending Ascot today or the party political debate on the European election, M'Lord."

Daily Express, June 19, 1984

"I'm in no mood for jokes about Tory wets!"

Daily Express, October 9, 1984

"Only one thing will keep this off the front page – if your wife came in with the Chancellor of the Exchequer.

Daily Express, January 29, 1987

"I don't suppose Mr Gorbachev's plan to remove nuclear missiles from Europe will do anything to improve our TV reception."

Daily Express, March 3, 1987

"Never misses the chance to give her slightly less than centre politics an airing."

Daily Express, March 12, 1987

"The old girl who kept us up all night trying to make us vote for her candidate – she gone?"

Daily Express, April 14, 1987

"Yes, I did read that Maggie was sending in the girls."

Daily Express, October 1, 1987

"Thanks to Judge Pickles the cleaners are putting in for a 10 per cent rise – it takes longer to clean up after a dinosaur than a judge."

Sunday Express, January 21, 1990

"Dad handed in his war medals in protest against the Poll Tax but the Corporal told him to take them home and clean 'em up."

Sunday Express, March 11, 1990

"I expect you will be getting your papers to rejoin the Bengal Lancers any day now, Colonel."

Sunday Express, August 12, 1990

Yuletide Greetings

"I should avoid asking things like What do they think of their first Christmas under a Tory Government?"

Daily Express, December 19, 1951

"They don't sound like the words on that nice little Christmas card you sent us."

Daily Express, December 28, 1962

"I fear a lot of mummies and daddies are going to get LP Beatle records for Christmas."

Daily Express, December 12, 1963

"I said it's a good time to get your foot stuck in a chimney with the fireman still out."

Daily Express, December 24, 1977

"He's first in the queue for the after-Christmas Sale. Sugar meece down half-price."

Daily Express, December 21, 1978

"Does Madam realise she's either introducing him to a life of untold riches or the life of a lightweight pug?"

Daily Express, November, 1986

Spot the Difference

Find 10 differences between this picture and the one on the page opposite.

Answers can be found on the final page of this book

Daily Express, August 29th, 1951

Daily Express, August 29th, 1951

Spot the Difference Answers

October 3, 1962

August 29, 1951

November 11, 1958

The publisher wishes to thank Derek Unsworth for his assistance in compiling this collection.

Editor's Note:

Because we wanted to include cartoons that have never been seen in any of the previous Giles annuals, we have used images from our newspaper archive. You will find, as a result, that there is a variation in the reproduction of the cartoons but hope you enjoy these uncovered delights.